GEORGINA AND T[HE DRAGON]

A Pantomime

Synopsis:

Georgina is set somewhere else. A fearsome dragon, called Keith, is ravaging the land. The King sends a hero to kill the beast but his progress is slow, and so Georgina, the King's daughter, heads off as well. The King's Tax Collector is also in pursuit but his aim is to protect the dragon so that it will continue to steal and destroy, thereby forcing the King to collect more taxes and so securing his own future.

The Good Group is captured by Robbers who eventually decide to help. Georgina meets a Witch and gets a lethal dragon potion, which has a strange effect on humans. And so everyone converges on Dragon Mountain as the story reaches it's thrilling and unexpected climax.

Cast List

The King
Keith, *the Dragon*
The Chancellor
Jinx, *the Jester*
The Dame
Tax Collector
Chester
Georgina
Cuthbert
Derek
Boris
The Witch
Dobbin
Tray-cey

1st Robber
2nd Robber
3rd Robber
1st Peasant
2nd Peasant
3rd Peasant
Knights
Peasants
Dancers
Street Vendors etc.

THE SET

Panto style, requires a castle, a forest, a cave and various "on the road" scenes.

PROLOGUE *(Epic music).*

Peasant: Long, long ago and far, far away there was a kingdom peopled almost entirely by happy peasants, content to work in the fields, collect in their crops and pay their taxes to the King.
Sadly these happy times were not to last, for a terrible scourge swept the land in the form of a fearsome dragon, a dragon with scales of iron, breath of fire, horrible flashing eyes and terrible gnashing teeth. A dragon called .... Keith. He flew from plain to plain beating his mighty wings, casting a terrible shadow and causing great panic and dread in the previously happy towns and villages of the kingdom. The only person who was pleased was the King's tax collector because it meant he had plenty of work. *(Tax Collector smirks at AUDIENCE).*

One day in the ancient city of Milton Keynes....

Lights up to reveal a Medieval Fair, the KING is on his throne surrounded by a small crowd. There is music playing and a folk dance is in progress.

King: *(as dance finishes to polite applause).....* and I was surrounded by at least one hundred bloodthirsty bandits, and what did I do? I....

Crowd: *(as one - bored).* Killed the lot of them.

King: Oh, yes.... fine.... Oh!, did I tell you about the vicious dragon of Eastbourne?

Crowd: Yes, you killed it!

King: The wild boar of Basingstoke?

Crowd: Yes, you killed it!

King: And was I afraid?

Crowd: No! *(there is a loud roar offstage).*

Everybody: Aargh! A dragon!.... It's Keith! *(There is a general panic and everyone runs into everyone else as they flee. When the stage is empty, KEITH saunters in. He is a dragon but small, cool (dark glasses), unthreatening and carrying an ipod. He looks around and realises that nobody is there. He goes to pick up the gold then suddenly sees the AUDIENCE. He panics momentarily, then he points the ipod at them and presses PLAY. A pathetic roar results. KEITH stares at them pointedly, then slides forward looking cute).*

Keith: You didn't run away! Everybody always runs away, that's why I've taken to roaring and raging and things, because no-one ever talks to me anyway. Will you be my friends?.... Will you *(Talon to ear)*. Oh thank you. I'm not really a bad dragon, I'm just a beast who is misunderstood, beneath these scales you'll find only good.... Oh this is nice, now I've got loads of friends *(consults watch)*. Oh dear, I've got to go, sorry I'm going to the dentist, healthy fangs are so important for an active dragon.... Bye! *(KEITH exits carrying gold)*

ACT I

SCENE 1.
The Castle, some time later.

On stage we have the KING looking miserable, the ROYAL CHANCELLOR and JINX the JESTER who is wearing headphones. There are also various Courtiers.

King: *(depressed).* This just can't go on, the treasury is empty, the streets are deserted, the crops are rotting in the fields, the grain is rotting in the warehouses and the Cabinet haven't got a clue what to do...again!

We must find a way to get the treasure and dispose of that dragon. Call the bravest knights in all the land, including Arnie.

Off Stage 1: Call the bravest knights in all the land, including Arnie.

Off Stage 2: Arnie's not here.

Off Stage 1: Why not?

Off Stage 2: His contract's been terminated, but he did say "I'll be back." *(As the AUDIENCE roar with uncontrolled laughter there is a trumpet call. A group of KNIGHTS rush in brandishing spears and looking brave and tough. JINX is reading a Beano and paying no attention).*

King: That was quick.

Chancellor: Yes, Sire, they were waiting in the wings for their moment of glory.

King: Good, because this is it. Brave Knights.

Knights: Sire!

King: This is your greatest moment! Fame and glory await you, fabulous riches and a glamorous lifestyle are just around the corner. *(They are looking more and more enthusiastic, but as the King describes the task they slink off one by one until there is nobody left - except JINX).*

To earn these startling rewards, all you must do is trek through leagues of robber infested forest, wade through mighty rivers, cross frozen wastes and climb tortuous cliffs in search of Keith, the tragic dragon, who lives by the sea. This beast is ferocious, dangerous, ugly, warty and worst of all he's got bad breathe. Here's a picture.

A child's drawing of a Dragon is projected onto the wall. The KING turns to where the KNIGHTS were). Now! What, where have they gone? The cowards! They've fled. What sort of knights are these? Cancel their overtime! Halve the night rate! Cut off their allowances! *(He sees JINX).* Ah, one left, there may still be some hope. Ho, varlet,..... Jester.... Jinx.... Are you listening to me? *(JINX is nodding his head to music. He is really rocking. The KING angrily removes the headphones and the tune from a Children's Cartoon is heard.*

Jinx: Oi! I was listening.... to.... that your Royal Highness, not that it matters of course your brightness, your Majesticness, your wittiness, your gloriousness.

King: Jinx?

Jinx: Yes your Majesty?

King: Shut up!

Jinx: Certainly your Majesty. At once your Majesty.

King: That's better. *(JINX opens his mouth. The KING raises a finger and an eyebrow).* Jinx, you will have to kill the dragon.

Jinx: But....

King: It's all right, there's no need to thank me.

Jinx: But....

King: It's a big responsibility for a lad like you.

Jinx: But....

King: But I have every faith in you. Well, I have some faith in you. Well you might do it.... Oh you'll have to do. Go and get a sword and be off by dawn.

Jinx: But my mother doesn't like me going off by myself.

King: Hmm, good point.... I have an idea!

Jinx: You do? I mean you do!

King: Yes, your Mother can go with you.

Jinx: You have got to be joking!

King: What do you mean?

DAME enters.

Dame: Ohh helloo yur Kingliness, hello boys and girls. No, no that will never do, you should say "hello gorgeous". Let's practise. Hello boys and girls! Wonderful, now where was I? Oh yes, hello your Kingliness, you look so cute today with that little crown and all those twiddly furry bits.

King: Get off me woman! Unhand me I say!

Dame: Don't be so touchy!

King: I could make the same request of you, madam! Now Jinx, you'd better tell her about the trip.

Dame: Oh that's all right, you don't need to bother I overheard everything and I'd love to go and so would Jinx, we would be honoured to serve our King and Country in this way.

King: And to get the money.

Dame: *(huffily).* I beg your pardon.

King: I said "AND TO GET THE MONEY"

Dame: How did you know?

King: Telepathy?

Dame: Ooh, I like that in a man.

King: Hmm. I have decided to give you the fastest horse in the Kingdom! Dobbin!

Sound FX of galloping horse, screeching of brakes. DOBBIN enters.

Jinx: That old mule!

King: Take it or leave it.

Jinx: I'll leave it.

Dame: Ahh *(encouraging children)* don't be mean. I'll have it, it'll save my bunions. *(HORSE panics and flees followed by DAME, running. JINX exits looking dejected and the KING returns to his throne, shaking his head).*

King: Hopeless. Quite hopeless.

BLACKOUT

Lights up a little as the KING'S TAX COLLECTOR crosses Stage at centre.

K/T: And just in case it isn't, I'm going to follow them. Heh heh.

BLACKOUT

SCENE 2.
The Castle two weeks later.

The KING is on his Throne looking bored, GEORGINA sits near him. The CHANCELLOR is there, as are various others. They are all half asleep. A replacement JESTER is "Entertaining" them, playing a lute badly and singing.

Chester:

(Chorus) I am a jolly jester

And jesting is my game

I am a jolly jester

And Chester is my name.

> He strums his lute. An offensively loud burst of Rock Music or some such is blasted over the speakers. Everyone jumps. CHESTER smiles at AUDIENCE then turns to the KING with a straight face and continues. Each verse could end in the same way with a very different tune.

My job is to amuse you

With jokes and songs and quips

Causing endless merriment

On Tuesdays and on ships.

    Oh.

Chorus.

I started as a schoolboy

Entertaining all my friends

Wearing platform shoes and dufflecoats

And setting all the trends.

    Oh.

Chorus.

I went to jester training school

To improve my expertise

But I had to leave the second day

'Cos I couldn't pay my fees.

Oh.

Chorus.

Halfway through the last Chorus the KING hits him over the head with something heavy and he falls over. He gets up, rubs his head and continues.

Chester: Why did the monkey fall out of the tree?

King: I don't know and I don't really care.

Chester: Because he lost his grip

King: He's not the only one.

Chester: What's green and pear shaped?

King: A pear.

Chester: What do you call a man with a spade on his head?

King: dug.

Chester: What do you call a spider without legs?

King: A raisin.

Chester: What's white and can't climb trees?

King: A FRIDGE.

Chester: What's brown and can't climb trees?

King: A fridge in a sack.

Chester: Oh. OK.... Ahh.... OK I've got another one. Why did the chicken....
cross the road? *(Everyone suddenly perks up and looks interested).*

King: Ahh.... Umm.... I don't know, why did the chicken cross the road?

Chester: Ahh.... I don't know either, I've forgotten. *(CHESTER is pelted with plastic fruit and flees the stage).*

King: Thank goodness for that. Right. Back to political matters. Where is that blithering idiot Jinx? He's been gone for two weeks and we've heard nothing from him and that horrible dragon Keith is still rampaging around the Kingdom. What's the world coming to if in this day and age you can't send a hero off to defeat something. Now in my young day Heroes knew how to be Heroes, there was none of this new fangled messing around with high tech solutions! Bash em with something big! That's what I say. It was good enough for my Father so it's good enough for me.

Georgina: Daddy?

King: Oh, if my Mother could....

Georgina: Daddy!

King: .... see me now.

Georgina: DADDY!!*!#

King: Georgina *(as if he's just seen her).* What do you want?

Georgina: Oh dearest Daddy, can I go, I can defeat the dragon. Daddy, can I? Can I go? Oh Daddy, Daddy.

King: No you cannot! Your Mother wouldn't like it. *(Everyone looks around as if some ogre is about to appear. In fact she never does).*

Georgina: Oh yes she would!

King: Oh no she wouldn't!

Georgina: *(encouraging AUDIENCE).* OH YES SHE WOULD! Etc.

King: Thats's enough of that *(to AUDIENCE).* Peasants! Now you can't go and that's the end of that.

Georgina: If you don't let me go I'll, I'll, I'll....

King: Yes?

Georgina: .... I'll scream and scream until I'm sick in your wellies!

King/Chancellor: *(to AUDIENCE).* Eeurgh!

King: Oh all right then go. *(aside).* and good riddance!

Chancellor: *(aside).* Quite right. *(GEORGINA stamps on the CHANCELLOR'S toes).*

King: *(jumping aside).* That's enough of that. If you're going, go, but don't tell your mother.

Georgina: I won't. Oh thank you Daddy. *(Big wet kiss and rushes off).*

King: OK Chancellor, break open the wine gums, even if she doesn't get the dragon, there's a fair chance that the dragon will get her.

BLACKOUT

SCENE 3.
Somewhere in the Forest.

The King's TAX COLLECTOR enters, dressed in black and carrying a big sack marked SWAG.

K/T: Don't you hiss at me! *(whatever the AUDIENCE does).* Yes you did, don't deny it. Look! He's doing it again! *(Pointing at small child).* Yes, you, don't you laugh at me. *(Improvise as required).* I didn't want to be the King's Tax Collector, spending all my time taking money off old ladies and sweets off children. *(Pulls catapult).* Gimme all your sweets. You see what I mean? My job description says I have to be horrible for at least eight hours a day. No, I didn't want to be the King's Tax Collector. I wanted to be a landscape gardener specializing in rhododendrons! Or failing that, an (Opera singer, Song and Dance man, or whatever the character can handle. There is an opportunity here to insert a short routine). Unfortunately my mother was a witch and my father was a bank robber, so I had no choice and now I have to stop Jinx killing Keith the fearsome dragon, or the King won't need to collect any more taxes and I'll be out of a job.

Jinx: *(off stage)* This is the way I think.

K/T: Oh no, here they come, I'll quickly set a trap. They won't know I've been following them so they're bound to fall for it. *(He sets up some kind of Trap. Ideally this should eventually drag GEORGINA into the air. It could though be a pathetic loop of rope which picks one foot off the floor causing Georgina to look disdainfully at it. HE/SHE then hides. JINX and DAME enter with DOBBIN).*

Jinx: I'm sure this is the way!!

Dame: It can't be the way, there's no signpost.

Stagecrew: Oh Sorry!. *(Brings on a Signpost and smiles in an embarrassed way at the AUDIENCE).*

Jinx: *(grandly).* Thank you, my man *(gives him something).*

Stagecrew: A sweet! I don't want a measly sweet.

Jinx: OK, have the whole packet.

Stagecrew: Skinflint. *(Throws sweets into the AUDIENCE and walks off stage taking the Signpost).*

Jinx: Well, that's gratitude for you. Today's Youth, I don't know.

Dame: Oh Jinx! Now look what you've gone and done.

Jinx: What did I do?

Dame: You made him take the signpost away. Now we'll never get there.

Jinx: Never mind, we don't need no schmelly signpost, do we Dobbin? *He takes out a large map and looks at it. It has MAP written on it on the AUDIENCE'S side and it is upside down. After a moment consulting with Dobbin, he lowers the map. Looking up he sees the AUDIENCE and is obviously startled).* Where the Arrgh did they come from?

Dame: They're the Audience you stupid boy! *(She hits him around the head).* They've come to enjoy the show. Haven't you Boys and Girls? Etc...

Jinx: Oh, can I ask them a question then?

Dame: Can he Boys and Girls?.... Go right ahead.

Jinx: I know it sounds silly, but are we being followed? Etc. *(Ending with)* So, we are being followed., we'd better keep moving then. Come on then, off we go. Thanks for your help Mr. & Mrs. Audience. Bye.

K/T: *(Emerging from hiding).* Oh drat and double drat, and don't you hiss at me. I missed them.

Georgina: *(Off stage)* Come on Cuthbert!

K/T: Rats! Who's this? And there's no time to take my trap down. *(He hides). (GEORGINA stomps on, followed by CUTHBERT with a huge sack).*

Georgina: Well that's not fast enou.... Yelp! *(The trap is sprung and she is hanging from the top).* Help! Help!

K/T: Oh no! I've captured the Princess Georgina. Arrghh. *(He runs off stage).*

Georgina: Who was that? Cuthbert! Get me down from here! {Or out of here.}

Cuthbert: I'm sorry Ma'am, cutting down Princesses from cleverly concealed booby traps is not part of my duties. My union wouldn't like it. *(He sits down and takes out a newspaper).*

Georgina: Cuthbert, I'll get you for this.

BLACKOUT

SCENE 4.
Elsewhere in the Forest.

DAME and JINX enter with DOBBIN.

Dame: Hello Boys and Girls etc.

Jinx: Ahhhhh Choooo! .... Ah, Ah, Ah Chooooo! *(Falls over. Blown off his feet by the force of the sneeze).*

Dame: Oh, my little baby. My poor little sweetie pie. Is Jinxy Winxy catching a cold?

Jinx: No, I'm allergic to....

Dame: Now don't you worry pumpkin, mummikins is here with a qualification in pastoral first aid and a fully equipped castle expedition medical kit. *(She produces a large pair of pliers etc. JINX is backing off).* Dobbin! Get him! *(There is a brief chaos, ending with JINX being grabbed and thrown behind a bush. DAME is there, producing various bits and pieces. The sequence ends with JINX emerging covered in bandages and slings and so forth).*

Jinx: But Mother, I only sneezed.

Dame: Well you never can be too sure in this day and age and it's better to be safe than sorry. Now then, where are we?

Jinx: In the forest! *(DAME glares at him).* I'm not being very helpful am I mum? Do you think you can find our way?

Dame: Um, no. BUT I KNOW A MAN WHO CAN. *(Enter MAP SELLER).*

Map Seller: Maps! Maps for sale! Get your maps here. Finest quality, water resistant, user friendly cartographic aids. Dragon's lair clearly indicated.

Dame: You see? It never fails. Excuse me my good man, could I please have a
     map with a clearly marked "YOU ARE HERE" facility?

Map Seller: Certainly Mam, there you go. *(DAME holds it the wrong way up. MAP SELLER corrects her, raises eyebrows to AUDIENCE and leaves).*

Maps! Maps for sale! Etc.

Dame: Now then....

Jinx: Shh! Someone's coming.

Dame: *(Loudly).* PARDON DEAR?

Jinx: *(Shouting).* I SAID SHH! Oh never mind.

Dame: Yes dear.... What's that noise?

Jinx: What noise?

Dame: That noise. It sounds like a Welsh male voice choir.

Jinx: No, I don't....

Dame: Or is it the wind blowing mysteriously through the ancient oaks?

Jinx: No, I don't....

Dame: Or could it be....

Jinx: MOTHER! It's a band of robbers. Hide! *(There is panic as they all rush around, diving into hiding places. The ROBBERS enter, singing).*

Robbers: We are a band of robbers bold
                 We live here in the forest
                 Eating and drinking and robbing around
                 Led by our Chieftain called Boris.
                 Oh, Ho, Ho Ho and Hee Hee Hee (Lots of back slapping).

                 We are a band of robbers tired
                 'Cos we have been a-carryin'
                 A big old heavy wooden cage Containing the Maid Marion
                 Oh, Yo Ho Ho and Hee.....

Derek: Er Excuse me, excuse me.... BE QUIET! *(Everyone stares at him. He is very big).* I'm sorry Boris sir, but it doesn't work.

Boris: What do you mean it doesn't work? Of course it works. All right I accept the metre is a bit strained in places and one or two of the lads are a bit flat, but generally speaking I think that that was a very successful musical moment! It went down very well on Britain's Got Talent. Sort of.

Derek: Even so, IT DOESN'T WORK!

Boris: All right, don't get over excited, there's no need to shout, we're not in Parliament. Now, why doesn't it work?

Derek: *(Patiently).*
Because...we...haven't...captured...Maid...Marion.

Boris: Oh.... So, what is her name?

Derek: I don't know but I know this isn't the Maid Marion.

Boris: How?

Derek: The Maid Marion doesn't live in Essex.

Boris: And this one does?

Derek: Yes.

Boris: Oh! right then I'll ask her then. Oi! You in the cage. What's your name?

Tracey: Maid Tray-cey. Actor, dancer, singer and all-round showbiz performer.
   (Sings "There's no business like Show business" etc).

Boris: OK. Thank you. That's quite enough of that, oh rats!

Derek: So. Ah, shall we try it again sir?

Boris: Yes, I suppose so. Ready Men? 1, 2, 3, 4

Robbers: *We are a band of robbers tired*
               'Cos we've been a-carryin'
               A big old heavy wooden cage
               Containing the Maid Tray-cey

Boris: Fine. Happy now Dweeb? We'll camp here tonight. *(They settle down to sleep, the lights fade and there are some huge snores. JINX, DAME and DOBBIN look over the bushes).*

Dame: Hello Boys and Girls, Shh etc.

Jinx: *(Stage Whisper)* They've captured the Maid Tracey. We'll have to rescue her.

Dame: Oh Jinx must we? This isn't that sort of quest.

Jinx: What sort of quest?

Dame: You know.... Well perhaps you don't. *(JINX looks very puzzled).* All right we'll rescue her, but she'll have to come with us, we can't waste any more time. *(They creep on, stepping over various ROBBERS. JINX begins to sneeze. DAME blocks his nose, TRACEY blocks his nose and DOBBIN blocks his nose, but eventually he sneezes. The ROBBERS are awoken, there is a struggle and they are all captured, tied up and threatened with several nasty objects - e.g. a watering can).*

Boris: So! You'd try and steal our Tracey would ya! *(Long John Silver)* Well it be no good, oh ahh, oh ahh.

Derek: Sir, once again and hopefully for the last time! You are not Long John Silver.

Boris: How do you know?

Derek: Well, you have two legs, not the one one would normally expect. *(BORIS quickly stands on one leg).* You haven't got a parrot. *(BORIS produces a parrot).* And you get seasick in the bath.

Boris: Oh! All right then! Can I be Robin Hood?

Derek: No.

Boris: King Arthur?

Derek: No.

Boris: The Chancellor of the Exchequer?

Derek: N.... Well.... No.

Boris: OK, Boris the Bold it is! Now then you sniveling band of pusillanimous
prisoner snatchers, who are you?

Jinx: I am Jinx, Jester to his Majesty the King.

Dame: And I am Doris, his mother.

Boris: The King's Mother?

Dame: No, silly. HIS MOTHER! *(Pointing at JINX - there is romance in the
air - then he sees DOBBIN).*

Boris: And who, or what is this?

Jinx: That's Dobbin, our heroic steed!

Boris: He doesn't look very heroic to me. *(DOBBIN bites him).* Oww! He bit me!

Dame: Well. You were being unkind. Poor old Dobbin!*(Encourage Children).* Ahh. Nasty old Boris. Booo!

Boris: Don't be like that I'm quite nice really.

Dame: Booo!

Boris: You can Booo! all you like, I don't care, 'cos I'm well 'ard. Now where was I? Oh yes, you, what's your business in this 'ere forest?

Jinx: My business is no business of yours EVIL ROBBER! *(BORIS kicks him)* Oowww!

Boris: Have a care little jester, *(BORIS is very small).* They don't call me Boris the Bad for nothing.

Robber 1: No you have to pay them! Ha, Ha. *(BORIS kills him).* Farewell, cruel world. Urrghh!

Dame: If you must know, we're off to kill the most ferocious dragon in the Kingdom.

Boris: You don't mean.... Keith?

Dame: Yes! *(Sound FX Da Da Daaahh! and they all draw back, horrified).*

Boris: Team Talk! *(All the ROBBERS huddle to one side).* If they are tough enough to tackle Keith, then we'd better be nice to them.

Derek: You're right and if we let them go and they succeed, we'll be the only plunderers in the land. We'll be rich!

Boris: He hah. Good thinking Derek.

Robber 3: *(Looking across).* But they don't look very tough. *(They all turn and stare. The Others look back and smile).*

Boris: You're right *(looking depressed).* Perhaps we'd better go with them and lend a helping hand, or sword or something.

Derek: Yes.

Robber 3: Yes.

Boris: Right, *(to JINX).* Noble and jolly jester Jinx.... we, the Black Forest Gang, have decided to accompany you on your quest to free the land of Keith the Tragic Dragon, who lives by the sea. Who frolics in the autumn mist....

Jinx: Yes, yes, yes, well thank you very much, shall we leave immediately or would now be better?

Boris: Now sounds fine. Come on men! To Nottingham!

Derek: No! *(Bored).*

Boris: Oh...Oh...Oh...Oh.. let's just go. *(BORIS exits, running).*

Jinx: To the village beneath Dragon Mountain!

All: Hooray!
(They all exit. Enter THE KING'S TAX COLLECTOR).

K/T: Don't you hiss at me, I've warned you before. I'll have your pocket money! Etc. etc. This is getting worse and worse. Not only have I failed so far to stop Jinx, but I've succeeded in trapping the Princess Georgina, and Jinx has joined up with Boris the Bad. All is not lost, however, as I have, by way of Wikileaks, discovered the lair of Keith, and when they get there they will find my plans carefully laid. Hee Hee Ho Ho Ho Hum Hum. *(Exits and returns)* Hee!

BLACKOUT

SCENE 5.
Music in the western heroic style, or some such. The Village beneath Dragon Mountain. A deserted street.

Our merry band of heroes enter running from the other side of the stage.

All: Ahh Ha! *(They stop and look around, confused).*

All: Ahh Ha!

Dame: Well, I don't know. I was expecting a bit more of a welcome than this! *(To AUDIENCE).* What about you lot? Good! That helps anyway.

Jinx: Yes, are you sure this is the place? It looks like a ghost town. You never could read maps. Come to that, you never could read. *(DAME hits JINX).*

Dame: Well at least I can ride a horse.

Jinx: Only if it is going in a straight line.

Dame: *(Smack round head).* It's not my fault if the chapter on cornering got lost in the post.

Dobbin; Oh do be quiet both of you! *(There is a stunned silence).*

Jinx: It spoke.... Did it speak?.... Gulp!

Boris: All right, all right, calm down, calm down. When you two have quite finished.

Derek: This is the place. Look! There's a sign. *(Sign is held in from wings with silly name on it or name of town in which performance is taking place).*

Boris: Hmm, so where are all the people? Cooeee, cooeee. Oh come out, come out wherever you are!

Peasant 1: *(in hiding).* Why don't you leave us alone?

Peasant 2: *(in hiding).* Yes, we have nothing left, what with the high cost of living. the knock-on effect of the Banking crisis and the dragon an' all.

Peasant 3: The Bailiffs are coming tomorrow.

Jinx: But we are here to help.

Peasant 1: Yourselves, yes we know, we've heard it all before. Haven't we lads?

Rest: Yes, we have!

Peasant 1: And we've had enough. Haven't we lads?

Rest: Yes, we have!

Jinx: No.... But

Rest: No buts, we have had enough.

Boris: Bu....

Peasant 1: That's it, I've had it. Prepare to die! *(The PEASANTS run in and attack them. They are truly pathetic and soon end up on the floor. This doesn't shut them up).*

Peasant 1: *(Bloodily)* Well. What have you got to say for yourselves now?

Jinx: We come here to....

Peasant 2: Don't interrupt. You can't deny it.

Dame: Please listen, we....

Peasant 3: *(With large sword up nose).* Let's kill them!

Boris: Shut up! *(They fall silent. PEASANT 1 is muttering).*

Peasant 1: It's always the same, we never get to win. I don't like *(Blah Blah etc. BORIS goes over and threatens him with a sword. Each time he goes, the PEASANT starts again. Finally BORIS knocks him out).*

Jinx: We were sent here to protect you from the dragon.

Derek: We are the magnificent se.... *(He counts them and says the number there are).* and a half. *(DOBBIN)*

Peasant 2: Oh.

Peasant 3: I suppose that changes things.

Dame: I should hope it does. Now, where's the food, I'm ravished by hunger.

Derek: I should make the most of it!

Dame: What was that?

Derek: I said "I hope there's a roasted bit."

Peasant 3: Don't worry, there's as much tapioca as you can eat and after that, mushy peas. Now, bring on the dancing girls. Let's celebrate! *(Any music at all. Something Flamenco perhaps).*

Jinx: And now that we have eaten well, drunk well and been so wonderfully entertained, let us sleep, for tomorrow we go to the dragon's cave!

BLACKOUT

INTERVAL

ACT II

SCENE 1.
Setting is as ACT I, scene 3.

GEORGINA is still hanging from the tree. CUTHBERT is still reading a newspaper.

Georgina: *(Wheedling)* Cuthbert?

Cuthbert: Yes, M'Lady?

Georgina: If you get me down, I'll.... I'll....

Cuthbert: You'll what, M'Lady?

Georgina: I'll buy you a new train for your train set.

Cuthbert: Really, M'Lady? How generous.

Georgina: And... You can have that jacuzzi you've always wanted.

Cuthbert: Yees....

Georgina: And I'll cut you into the Dairy, free!

Cuthbert: Done, M'Lady. *(CUTHBERT springs into life and gets GEORGINA down. She brushes herself down and turns to the AUDIENCE).*

Georgina: It's amazing what people will do for a slice of the Dairy, free. *(Pause for gales of laughter and spontaneous displays of unbridled mirth).* Now, what day is it?

Cuthbert: *(Says whatever day it happens to be).*

Georgina: Oh drat! We'll never catch up with Jinx and the others now and they'll have all the fun of dealing with the dragon.

Cuthbert: I'd hardly call it fun Ma'am.

Georgina: Don't be so soppy Cuthbert. Hmm. What we need is a plan.

Cuthbert: Yes Ma'am. *(GEORGINA adopts a thoughtful pose. Sound FX of clocks ticking, things whirring and finally bells ringing).*

Georgina: I know! We'll use magic!

Cuthbert: Excellent Ma'am. Except for one small point.

Georgina: Yes?

Cuthbert: We don't know any magic.

Georgina: Ah. Oh well. Never mind, something will come up. You know, I really could do with a bite to eat. Any ideas?

Cuthbert: Would M'Lady care for some fish and chips?

Georgina: Splendid idea but where are we going to get them from? *(Enter wandering Fish and Chip man with sandwich board, portable deep fat fryer and dangling plastic fish. He comes with his own Queue to create the illusion of success).*

Cuthbert: How about him Ma'am?

Georgina: *(startled).* Goodness me where did that come from? Never mind it's just what we need. *(Barging past Queue)* OK then, make way for the Princess Georgina. *(To Man in front).* That goes for you as well, understand? Good. Now move!

Man: Have you got two pence to spare Miss?

Georgina: That's "Princess" actually and I don't give to beggars so buzz off! *(To FISH MAN).* Oy, you, Peasant. I want two portions of fish and chips, a large fizzy drink and a small glass of water for Cuthbert here and make it snappy.

Fish Man: *(Looking flustered).* OK, OK, keep your wig on Missus.

Georgina: *(Shouting).* HOW DARE YOU! I HAVE NOT GOT A WIG ON. I'LL REPORT YOU ON TRIPADVISOR AND THEN YOU'LL BE IN TROUBLE! *(She collects food).*

Fish Man: Oh No, please don't, I've worked so hard to build up my own little business against all the odds and one bad comment on TRIPADVISOR could be the end!

Georgina: Oh all right then, I'll be nice, for once, but I sincerely hope the chips aren't greasy! *(They sit on a bench and begin to eat. Everyone else exits).*

Georgina: *(Mouth full. Mumbles unintelligably).*

Cuthbert: Pardon Ma'am?

Georgina: *(As before).*

Cuthbert: Madam, you are making even less sense than you normally do.

(GEORGINA glares at him).

Georgina: *(Swallowing theatrically).* I said, "How the heck are we going to kill this blasted dragon."

Cuthbert: Well.... I daresay that a solution can and will be found.... One moment Ma'am, what's that on your newspaper?

Georgina: A speck of dirt? Right, I shall complain immedia....

Cuthbert: No, No, M'Lady, you remember your idea about using magic?

Georgina: Yes.

Cuthbert: Well look. *(GEORGINA holds up her paper, spilling her chips on the floor).*

Georgina: My chips!

Cuthbert: Never mind about that Ma'am, look at this.

Georgina: That's an advert for double-glazing, you stupid butler.

Cuthbert: Madam! Not that advert, this advert. Read it please, dear child. *(Said as if he'd like to wring her neck).*

Georgina: *(Reading aloud)* "Witch Mizerabelle Services. All the spells you need. Contact me now for a spell for any occasion." So?

Cuthbert: So, we can contact her to get a spell to kill the dragon.

Georgina: Very good Einstein, but the stupid witch has forgotten to say how to contact her!

Cuthbert: Oh. Oh dear.

Georgina: *(Pleased to be one up).* Right, so how are we going to find this witch then.... Smartie? *(Suddenly the WITCH appears in a puff of smoke).*

Georgina: Poohie! What's that smell?

Witch: *(Cackling).* It's my new perfume. It's highly scented with skunk drops and bat droppings. Nice eh dearie?

Georgina: No it certainly is not! Who are you anyway?

Witch: Me? You mean you don't recognise me? I'm Witch Mizerabelle. Photographs allowed only from the left, autographs later. Weather permitting of course.

Georgina: But how did you know that we wanted your services.

Witch: Secretly embedded voice activated hyperlink dearie, it's all the rage.

Georgina: And don't call me dearie.

Witch: Yes, Dearie.

Georgina: *(Glares).* Right we need a spell to....

Witch: Spells? Oh I have loads of spells. Spells in my pockets, spells up my nose, spells in my fingers, spells in my toes. Spells for the winter, spells for the spring, spells for just about any old thing.

Georgina: Do you have a spell that will make my life even more exciting than Emmerdale?

Witch: Don't be silly dear, there are limits, but here is my list of services. *(She hands a long scroll to CUTHBERT who dons his silly reading glasses)*

Cuthbert: *(Frosty stare at the audience)* I BEG YOUR PARDON! *(He clears his throat)*

Ahem, errm.... Very interesting. Carpet cleaning, car-valeting, personalized shopping, company on expensive holidays. Ah, here's something that might do!

Georgina: *(Snatching it).* Where? Lemme see! Oh yes! Dragons dealt with in or out of their Den. Keith's a speciality. That's lucky!

31

Cuthbert: What Madam requires is a spell for the mortification of monstrous lizards by means of a calamitous chemical concoction. (*The WITCH looks confused*).

Georgina: A Dragon potion!

Witch: Dragon potion, well why didn't you say. Nothing easier. Ah *(consults book).* Ah yes, here we are. Now, where's my cauldron? *(Fumbles around and produces a tiny Pot).*

Georgina: It's not very big.

Witch: Appearances can be deceptive, you mark my words. Let's begin. I'll call out the ingredients and you bring them in. *(The Pot has a hole in the bottom into a hidden bowl. The WITCH uses a funnel).* First, atmosphere. *(Clicks fingers to get eerie light and sound).* Hmm. "A little bit of this." *(The others rush around collecting boxes with variuos powders which are poured into the cauldron).* And "A little bit of that." a pot, a pan, a broom and a hat. No No, cancel those, that's a different show. Ahh. Ray a drop of golden sun.

>   *(Sung):*   Now stir them all and pinch yourself,
>
>   Say Ha and now the spell is done!

> *(She produces a small phial of coloured liquid and gives it to GEORGINA).*

Georgina: Are you sure it will work?

Witch: Work? Of course it will work, but make sure you follow the instructions and don't take any yourself, the effect on humans could be very strange!

Georgina: The effect on humans could be very strange you say?

Witch: *(To AUDIENCE).* Yes the effect on humans could be very strange.... Got that.... Good.... Now off you go , don't get lost and don't forget what I've told you. *(They exit. The WITCH picks up the watch).* Hopeless. Quite hopeless. Oh well never mind.

BLACKOUT

SCENE 2.

At the foot of Dragon Mountain. Our heroes enter.

Dame: Hello Boys and Girls etc.

Tray-cey: How much further do we have to go? I'm totally thwaiped.

Jinx: We're nearly there, this is the foot of Dragon Mountain and according to Wikileaks, Keith's lair is half way up on the left hand side.

Boris: Well let's get on then. I can't stand hanging around before a fight. Let's get to it. They don't call me Boris the Brave for nothing. *(There is a tremendous roar. Everyone panics, rushes around and hides. After a short pause, KEITH strolls in carrying his Swag Bag.*

Keith: *(To AUDIENCE).* Hello Boys and Girls etc. I'm so happy to see you again, it's always nice to meet old friends. Would you like to see my swag? Yes? Good, look I've got all sorts of things. *(These are cheap gifts that Keith gives away - with appropriate dialogue).* There, that's enough of that for today. Oh dear I am tired, I think I'll take a little nap. Children, if anyone comes near will you be my alarm and shout as loudly as you can "Look behind you"? You will, oh thank you. *(There follows a sequence during which one or the other of our heroes creeps forward only to be forced back as the Children warn KEITH, who is always just that little bit too late to see them. Eventually they all rush him and KEITH is captured. He immediately bursts into floods of tears).*

Keith: Waaagghh!!! Waaaghh!!! WAAAGHHHH!! Sob, sob etc. *The Others all look perplexed. They huddle to one side of the stage).*

Boris: That can't be it surely, it's meant to be huge and fearsome and mean and nasty, with big nasty gnashing teeth.

Derek: Well it's definitely a dragon.

Jinx: Yes, but is it the right dragon? We can't go around capturing any old dragon, the King wouldn't like it

Dame: Let's ask it.

Tray-cey: But it might not tell the truth.

Derek: Don't be silly. Animals can't lie, only humans who are being naughty can do that.

Boris: Go on then ask it.

Derek: Why me? You're Boris the Big, you ask it.

Boris: Ahh, actually I think Jinx should ask it; after all he's the official dragon slayer.

Jinx: But it's not as if I wanted to be.

Dame: Oh for goodness sake, I'll ask it. Dragon, are you or are you not Keith?

Keith: Waaaghh!

Dame: Ohh, my poor little dragikins, don't be upset, no-ones going to hurt you.

(To others). Are you!

Others: No no no etc.

Dame: I can see now that it's all been a big misunderstanding and I'm sure that if you return all the money you've taken, the King will forgive you and you can come and live at the court and everything will end happily ever after and that goes for the Robbers too.

Robbers/Keith: Do you really think so?

Dame: Yes I do. Do you children? Etc.
    You see? Everybody thinks so.

Keith: Oh goody goody, let's go to my cave and have tea before we set off. It's been a bit of a long day what with one thing and another and such as like and all. *(They all exit as the curtains close and the Tax Collector appears on the apron).*

K/T: Don't you hiss at me! etc. It couldn't be worse. Not only has Jinx made friends with the dragon, but even Boris and his band of Baddies have turned over a new leaf. I'll have to retrain. I could end up in education. No, no, no it's too horrible to contemplate! I must think of a plan. I know, I'll disguise myself as Keith, sneak into his cave and be really unpleasant when the real Keith isn't there, then they'll run away and Keith will think they've deserted him and he'll start being ferocious and nasty again and all will be well. Hee Hee I'm so evil. Lucky I brought my fake dragon costume with me! *He exits to tremendous booing as CUTHBERT and GEORGINA enter from the back of the hall).*

Cuthbert: Madam. Madam. Please slow down. I'm not as young as I used to be.

Georgina: Stop whingeing Cuthbert, we're almost there, that's Dragon Mountain
            up ahead.

Cuthbert: Yes Ma'am. Thank you Ma'am.

Georgina: *(Relenting).* Oh all right Cuthbert we'll stop for five minutes whilst we plan what to do next.

Cuthbert: Yes Ma'am. Thank you Ma'am.

Georgina: Now, we know that Keith's cave is somewhere in the mountain, but where? It's very big and we don't know how much time we've got. That dolt Jinx could get there at any time, deal with the dragon and get all the glory.

Cuthbert: Not to mention the money.

Georgina: Hmm. I know, you go that way and I'll go this way and whichever of us finds the way will call the other with a secret call.

Cuthbert: What is the call Ma'am?

Georgina: I can't tell you that, it's a secret, and there might be somebody listening!

Cuthbert: Yes Ma'am. Thank you Ma'am.

Georgina: But I will write it down. Memorise this and then eat the paper.

>*(CUTHBERT does so with a look of extreme disgust).* Right, let's go.

>*Lights fade slightly as curtains open to reveal the interior of the dragon's lair.*

SCENE 3.
The Dragon's Lair.
All the good guys are sitting around. KEITH is pottering about being the host.

Keith: I'll just go and get some more tea. Won't be a tick. *(As he exits, CUTHBERT "Falls" into the scene looking flustered).*

Jinx: Cuthbert! What are you doing here?

Cuthbert: Bleeding actually.

Dame: Never mind Cuthbert dear, I do have my certificate in....

All: .... pastoral first aid and a castle expedition medical kit.

Cuthbert: Yes, thank you but I don't think that will be necessary, it's only a minor abrasion.

Dame: Oh. *(Disappointed. At this point KEITH enters).*

37

Cuthbert: Oh my goodness me! It's, it's, it's that, it's a dragon! *(KEITH is frightened).*

Jinx: Do stop yelling Cuthbert, you'll frighten him. Let me introduce you to Keith - Cuthbert. Cuthbert - Keith. Keith is coming back to Milton Keynes to start a new life, aren't you Keith?

Keith: Oh yes, and I'm really looking forward to it.

Cuthbert: You mean he isn't a bloodthirsty, fierce, ferocious, warty, ugly beast with bad breath after all?

Jinx: That's right. He's just a lovable lizard who's been given a bad press.

Cuthbert; Well that's a relief. For one moment there I thought I was going to be
       toasted!

Keith: You can be if you want to be.

Cuthbert: No!

Keith: To Cuthbert my newest friend.

All: To Cuthbert.

Dame: There, that was all right wasn't it?

Cuthbert: Sniff. I've never been toasted before. I'm deeply touched, thank you, thank you all.

Dame: That's all right, lovely. Now, let's eat. *(They eat).*

Cuthbert: Delicious buffet Keith.

Keith: Erm, nothing is too much trouble for my buddies. We are all buddies aren't we?

Jinx: Of course we are K....

Cuthbert: I don't know if I could allow myself to be referred to as a "buddy." Being a proper Butler you see.

Boris: Terribly sorry. Fwah, fwah, fwah.

Cuthbert: Huh! Some people might do well to consider how other people might view some people who make remarks that most people would think of as some people being rude.

Boris: Eh what? Is he insulting me? 'Cos if he is, I'll have 'im I will. Where's my sword?

Suddenly the King and the Lord Chancellor burst in.

Georgina: Daddy, what are you doing here!

King: You tell them Lord Chancellor.

Chancellor: Well, shortly after you left your MOTHER (*everyone looks around in a really worried way*) found out what was going on and she was REALLY, REALLY cross and you all no what that means (*everyone nods and shivers with fright*) and so the only thing for it was to use up some air-miles and get here as fast as we could to make sure everything ended Happily Ever After.

King: We had to fly ECONOMY, it was GHASTLY!

Chancellor: But we're here now and that's the main thing.

They notice Keith for the first time.

King / Chancellor: Eek! What's that?

Georgina: It's not a "what" it's a "who". It's Keith!

Chancellor: Really? That's Keith? The Keith? The warty fearsome nas...

Derek: Yes. Yes, we've been through all that, it's all been a big misunderstanding. Keith's giving everything back and we're all coming to live at the Palace.

King: Even if SHE is living there. (*Everyone looks around again.*)

Georgina: Even then, mum might like having another Dragon to talk to.

King: That could work, good thinking everyone.

Keith: Ahem. *(Cough).* Friends, friends, may I suggest a guided tour?

Cuthbert: Of what pray?

All: Urm.

Keith: My cave of course.

All: His cave of course.

Boris: Well....

Keith: This is only the day chamber, there's a lot more to see and it's all stacked with treasure. Please say you will.

Boris: Sounds good to me. *(Standing).*

Jinx: *(With mouth full).* Not just yet, we're busy.

Keith: Perhaps later then. Pass the cakes, Cuffy. *(Slaps him on the back).*

Cuthbert: What's the magic word?

Keith: Ermm.... Abracadabra? Alacazam? Pass the little round sponge cakes with a cream and jam filling, icing on the top and tons of hundreds and thousands, AS FAST AS YOU CAN!

Cuthbert: No, no, no it isn't....

Keith: *(To AUDIENCE).* Oh no, I didn't say it properly! Perhaps it wasn't loud enough! I don't suppose that there's a teensy weensy chance *(signals with fingers)* that you could help me?

Audience: Yes! Etc.

Keith: Oh goody! I'll put the words on the screen to help you! Ready? A one, a two, a one two three four. *(At this point CUM BAI YAH is broadcast loudly)* Boris. If you'd be so kind.

Boris: Certainly Keith. *(BORIS exits and there is a sound of mayhem. He re-enters).*

Keith: Thank you Boris.

Boris: My pleasure Keith.

Keith: Now then children. 1,2,3,4,.... etc.

Cuthbert: Good try, but not good enough.

Keith: Can't I just have one.... please! Pretty please.... Oh!

Cuthbert: All right then you can have one.

Keith: Don't want one now, anyway!

Cuthbert: Good because there aren't any left!

Jinx: That wasn't very nice was it Boys and Girls etc.... Do you want to come on this tour or what?

Cuthbert: Oh yes.... if I could! If it's at all possible.... I am sorry.... It's because I spend so much time with Georgina. She's such a bad influence. So if you don't mind, you don't, do you?

All: Yes.

Cuthbert: Good. Let's go this way. *(He exits. Nobody else moves).*

Keith: OK, The grand tour!

Jinx: I think we should go this way.

Dame: I vote for the scenic route. *(Improvise one line for each character on stage. They all go off in different directions. KEITH is last to go. CUTHBERT re-enters).*

Cuthbert: Oh dear they've all gone and I forgot to warn Keith about the Magic Potion. If you see him children, will you warn him? Thank you. Now, I must try and find the others. *(He exits. K/T enters. He is now identical to KEITH).*

K/T: Made it! Don't you hiss at me! Nobody will recognise me dressed up like this. Now all I need to do is find that jumped up Jester and that dappy Dame and that boring Boris and give them a real fright and then they'll all run away and Keith will go back to pillaging. Hee Hee, I'm so evil. *(He exits. GEORGINA enters in her battle gear and carrying the Potion. She sees the AUDIENCE).*

Georgina: OK you numbskulls, this is the plan! Do you agree that this dragon, poor excuse for one that he is, needs to be dealt with?

Audience: NO!

Georgina: I knew it! You've fallen for his simple ways and basic kindness! Well It's not going to stop me! Ah food, the ideal place to plant my magic potion. Now what shall I put it in, the cakes? No. The sandwiches? No. I know, the punch, then it will be certain to knock him out. Now I'll go and hide and wait for my trap to be sprung.

There next follows a sequence during which various characters wander/rush/ amble across the stage in the style of a French four door farce. This includes KEITH and K/T. Dialogue can include:-

"I'm sure I've been here before" "Halloooo"
"I knew I should have turned left." etc. etc.

Eventually K/T comes in mopping his brow. He goes toward the punch, almost drinks it, then doesn't and so on. Finally he does and there is a marvelously overdone transformation scene. As he is changing the other characters appear in the shadows. Everyone thinks it is KEITH and they are very sad. When he is finally still, everyone gathers round crying and sobbing.

GEORGINA springs in.

Georgina: Ah haa! So my plan has worked. Keith the fearsome, nasty, smelly, warty dragon is no more. Success!

Cuthbert: Madam, of all the nasty, stupid mean things you have done, this was certainly the worst.

Boris: Even I, Big, Brave Boris the Big and Bold have never done anything as blatantly bad as this. You really are horrible.

Dame: She is horrible, isn't she Boys and Girls. etc. etc.

Georgina: *(Sniff).* I really am sorry, I thought it was the right thing, but if he had so many friends, he can't have been bad. Oh I feel terrible.

Jinx: And so you should, oh how could you? *(GEORGINA bursts into tears).* So is he gone then?

Derek: I.... I think so. It's hard to tell.

Dame: He really was quite a character. *(Everyone is crying. KEITH enters from the back, sees everyone upset and begins to cry too).*

Keith: *(Sniff).* What's everyone crying about?

Dame: He's gone!

Keith: Who's gone?

All: You have. WHAT!!!!

Keith: All right don't shout like that, it's been a very emotional day!

All: You're all right!

Keith: Am I.

All: Yes!

Keith: *(Poking himself).* So I am. Fabulous isn't it?

Cuthbert: No need to exaggerate!

Jinx: But if you're Keith, which you are, who is this? Georgina, who did you give the potion too?

DAME removes the mask from K/T. He is wearing beads and round glasses and a hippy wig.

Dame; Why, it's the tax collector, I think, but he looks a bit different. He's coming around, he's going to be all right!

K/T: Oh, hey man, what's happening. Hey, here have some money.

Cuthbert: That witch said the potion would have a strange effect if taken by a human being and it certainly has!

Keith: Well all's well that ends well. The land is now happy and free. So let's have a really huge party.

Georgina: And all the food is on me!

Cuthbert: Huh?

All: Oh shut up Cuthbert!!!

BLACKOUT

THE END

Printed in Great Britain
by Amazon